D0578230

COURTYARDS

COURTYARDS

Intimate Outdoor Spaces

DOUGLAS KEISTER

Gibbs Smith, Publisher
Salt Lake City

FOR SANDY, ALWAYS

First Edition
09 08 07 06 05   5 4 3 2 1

Text and photographs © 2005 Douglas Keister

All rights reserved. No part of this book may be reproduced by any means whatsoever without written permission from the publisher, except brief portions quoted for purpose of review.

Published by
Gibbs Smith, Publisher
P.O. Box 667
Layton, Utah 84041

Orders: 1.800.748.5439
www.gibbs-smith.com

Designed by Maralee Lassiter
Printed and bound in Hong Kong

Library of Congress Cataloging-in-Publication Data

Keister, Douglas.
  Courtyards : intimate outdoor spaces / Douglas Keister.— 1st ed.
     p. cm.
  Includes bibliographical references.
  ISBN 1-58685-540-9
  1. Courtyards. I. Title.
  NA2858.K45 2005
  712'.6—dc22
                                2005008778

contents

ACKNOWLEDGEMENTS

Special thanks go to the homeowners who opened their homes and courtyards and to the organizations and individuals who provided information on courtyards in their areas:

SOHO San Diego; Tabitha Home, Lincoln, NE; Nebraska State Capitol Building; Barb and Tiffany at Lucas Lagoons Inc., Sarasota, FL; New Urban Builders, Chico, CA; Alexandra Rasic/Homestead Museum, Industry, CA; Jarrett Lobell/*Archaeology Magazine;* Gingerbread Mansion, Ferndale, CA; The Towers, Milford, DE; The Adamson House, Malibu, CA; The Cloisters, New York City; National Gallery of Art, Washington D.C.; Rob Boyd/B&W; Courtyards, New Orleans; Hubbell and Hubbell Architects, San Diego; Pat O'Brien's, New Orleans; Court of the Two Sisters, New Orleans; Colonial Williamsburg, VA; Kenneth and BeBe Adatto; Tari Lagasse; Louis and Judy Freeman; Louis and Ruthis Frierson; David and JoAnn Morgan; Paul Duchscherer; Brian Coleman; Arrol Gellner; Laverne and Roger Warner; Katherine Keister; Danny and Karen Leonetti; Brenda and Jim Cosby; Merrie Meckley; Michael Melhado; Donna Pickard; Carlo Marchiori; Tony Banthutham; Betsy Vosburgh; Chris Schweitzer; Sandra Simpson; Sally Schoeffel; Melinda Lee; John Prosen; Beth Callender; Brad Maxey; Bill W.; Michael Redmon; Charlotte Deane; Rebecca Grossenbacher; Tom Shess; Ted Bosley; Grace Kim; Mark West; Lynne Christenson; Joan Cudhea; Parker H. Jackson; Dennis Steensen; Tom and Jill Resk, James Mabry, Sarah Surber and Josh Brown.

Many thanks to my agent extraordinaire, Julie Castiglia; to publisher extraordinaire, Gibbs Smith, Publisher; and most of all to my wife, Sandy Schweitzer.

A very special thanks goes to Sandé Lollis, who scouted out sites and assisted with photography in San Diego. For scouting or assisting contact her at *SandeCrafts@aol.com.*

Additionally, in New Orleans, Louis J. Aubert (ASID) scouted locations and assisted on photo shoots. Louis is an excellent resource for design and color of all types of historic architecture. Contact him at (504) 861-0968 or *Mrcolour@aol.com.*

Stambouli

2

HISTORY OF THE COURTYARD

Few architectural elements are more closely associated with comfort, protection, and security than the courtyard—an outdoor living space that is partially or fully enclosed by walls or buildings. The courtyard became a major architectural design element almost as soon as humans began constructing permanent buildings.

Scholars tell us that courtyards have been around since at least 3000 BC. The earliest civilizations in China, the Middle East, and North Africa all had courtyards. Protection was the primary function of these early courtyards, with high walls providing a shield from the weather and a barrier to marauding animals and unwanted human visitors. In later western culture, the requirements of a courtyard were looser, and any area that was partially or entirely enclosed by walls or buildings could be called a courtyard.

Today, defining a courtyard seems to depend on the elements it contains and the feelings it evokes rather than the architecture that surrounds it. The basic elements of a courtyard have always been water, walls, and sky combined to convey qualities of intimacy, security, and quiet.

ANCIENT COURTYARDS

The best places to see true courtyards are in Middle Eastern and Chinese cities, the very places where civilization developed. The ancient Persians built many of their courtyards as miniature representations of Paradise. Each contained a water element—a fountain, well, or pool central to the courtyard design—that provided a soothing contrast to the parched lands beyond the courtyard's walls. Some of the earliest written references to courtyards are found in the Bible. In the book of Exodus, plagues of frogs, gnats, and flies invaded the usually serene Egyptian courtyards. The book of Esther contains a reference to a royal courtyard. A courtyard is used as shelter at night in both the books of

This vintage albumen photograph was taken by noted photographer Felix Bonfils around 1880 at Cour de la maison Stambouli, in the old city section of Damascus, Syria. The living quarters are arranged around the courtyard, which has a still fountain that at one time may have been a well. The two-story building with the balcony probably dates from the eighteenth century. The different kinds of stonework often used in the old courtyards can be seen on the house, the fountain, and the ground. There are black and white stripes of basalt and white stone, colored pastework on the frieze area and above the doors, and beautiful marble mosaics.

Tobit and Nehemiah, and Moses instructs the Israelites to build booths in their courtyards during the feast days of the seventh month. In all, courtyards are mentioned over a dozen times in the Bible and always in the context of walled enclosures.

ROMAN COURTYARDS

The eruption of Mount Vesuvius in AD 79 buried the Italian city of Pompeii and its hapless citizens in volcanic ash, making Pompeii the best place to study perfectly preserved examples of Roman courtyards. In the ancient Roman world, courtyard houses were referred to as atrium houses. Usually lined up shoulder to shoulder on the street, these homes had no windows, resulting in a rather uninteresting and tedious streetscape that belied the splendor beyond the high walls. Upon entering the home, a visitor might encounter an open-roofed room that contained an *impluvium*, a central pool that collected rainwater from the inward-slanted roof. This small courtyard-like room served as the entrance to the main house. In back of the main house, a formal courtyard often surrounded by Greek-style colonnades would form a peristyle. These peristyle courtyards were the templates for church courtyards, called cloisters, which developed centuries later.

CHINESE COURTYARDS

Courtyards have been a part of Chinese architecture for more than 5,000 years. In crowded Chinese cities, courtyards are treasured sanctuaries of privacy and tranquility amidst the chaos of the urban world. Chinese courtyards almost always contain a garden and a water feature. A traditional Chinese courtyard

There is no better place to observe the construction and configuration of ancient courtyards than Pompeii, Italy, a city perfectly preserved in volcanic ash during a violent eruption of Mount Vesuvius in AD 79. This is the courtyard at the House of Meleager, one of Pompeii's wealthier citizens. Thanks to an elaborate system of aqueducts constructed at the end of the first century BC, Pompeii had a generous water supply. What looks like a swimming pool here is actually a fishpond, aerated by a fountain at the center and a set of stairs at the far end. Its shape is dictated by a system of niches, which are positioned to provide shade for the fish. Lurking in the shadows is one of Pompeii's ubiquitous dogs, which show up every morning, adopt individual tourists, and accompany them as they trek through the ancient streets.

Many well-to-do citizens of Pompeii built atrium houses. The atrium (inner courtyard) of the House of the Amorini Dorati (Golden Lovers) was, as in most Roman houses, near the front. The courtyard was essentially a public area since it could usually be viewed from the street entrance. The roof above the atrium was built sloping inward, allowing rainwater to flow into a pool (impluvium), seen here at the bottom of the photograph, where it would then be diverted into tanks or carried off in buckets. On the walls, vibrant frescoes are applied to stucco-covered walls. The entire ensemble was designed to show off the homeowner's wealth and social standing. After waiting enough time in the atrium to soak up the ambiance, a visitor would be greeted by the owner and led into the main house.

One of the very best places to see and experience truly beautiful restored courtyards is at the Palace of the Alhambra in Granada, Spain. Inspired by Moorish architecture, construction on the Alhambra began in 1238, with most of the major elements completed by 1354. Its courtyards, fountains, pools, and delicate architectural elements have long represented the finest integration of architecture and landscaping. The most famous entrance to the Alhambra is the Puerto del Vino (Door of the Wine) (right), a classic courtyard entrance that only hints at the splendors beyond. Two of the finest courtyards are the Patio de los Leones (Courtyard of the Lions) (above), named for the fountain that is supported by a dozen lions, and the Patio de Arrayanes (Courtyard of the Myrtles) (upper right), named for the fragrant myrtles that once grew around its pool.

house was arranged with several individual houses around a square, with each house belonging to a different family member. Many houses were constructed with multiple courtyards to buffer the street noise.

The courtyards in the quadrangles, or *siheyuan*, of old Beijing, China, have become popular tourist attractions. Many of them are known as "four-in-one" courtyards because they were meant to house four generations in one compound. Constructed using a set of strict guidelines, a typical *siheyuan* is a rectangular compound with one-story houses lined up on the cardinal points with a courtyard in the middle. A pair of stone lions usually sit before a bright red door with a painted lintel. Anyone entering must step over a high wooden threshold, where a stone screen is encountered that blocks prying outside eyes and dispels evil spirits. A small passageway opens to an outer courtyard flanked by rooms to the east and west. In the past, these rooms served as kitchens and living quarters for servants. On the north end of the outer courtyard is the main house, facing south to capture as much light and warmth as possible. Upturned eaves on the main house provide shade in summer, and two passages on either side of the main house provide access to the inner courtyard. Rooms on each side of the inner courtyard were for married children and their families. This inner courtyard offered a haven for contemplation, as well as space for a garden and decorative plants, while the outer courtyard served more utilitarian purposes. Recently, an eight-bedroom *siheyuan* in Beijing listed on eBay for $5,800,000.

There are thousands of these compounds in Beijing, and many of these have been purchased by foreign investors. But, sadly, many others are being bulldozed to provide for large open and public spaces, which makes an ancient Chinese proverb particularly apt: "A courtyard common to all will be swept by none."

NORTHERN EUROPEAN COURTYARDS

In northern Europe, large courtyards were more common than small ones. One scholar speculated that courtyards in colder climates needed to be larger to allow more of the sun's warming rays to enter, while courtyards in warmer climates remained small so their high walls could block the sun's searing rays. For whatever reason, courtyards in northern Europe tended to be quite large and were almost always associated with castles and palaces. Really walled cities and squares, they were centers of commerce and fortresses for protection.

These large medieval courtyards were miniature cities containing shops, craftspeople, animals, and, most importantly, a well or cistern to provide a ready source of water. In times of siege, the populace from outlying areas would stream into the courtyard for protection—the architectural equivalent of circling the wagons.

Medieval European farmhouses also had courtyards consisting of four buildings, often with thatched roofs, arranged around a central utility area that served as a workspace and an enclosure for smaller animals. Frequently, a balcony-like elevated walkway ran around the perimeter of the courtyard.

The most accessible and best-preserved small courtyards in Europe were built within church cloisters. Originally constructed to provide private areas where monks and nuns could go for seclusion and meditation, nowadays many cloisters are open to the public. Generally, cloister courtyards were completely surrounded by multicolumned and

This tiny courtyard in the Gothic Quarter just off Las Ramblas in Barcelona, Spain, manages to maintain the essential character of a true courtyard despite its diminutive size. Completely surrounded by buildings, this little courtyard still has a small water element at the center, and today the fountain doubles as a receptacle for a small palm tree. According to Professor John S. Reynolds, who wrote the seminal book on Spanish courtyards (see Suggestions for Further Reading on page 151), courtyards in warm sunny climates like Barcelona tended to be small for a very practical reason: their petite size and high walls shield the courtyard from the searing rays of the sun. Conversely, Reynolds says that courtyards in cool northerly climes were usually larger, capturing more of the warming rays of the sun, which enter the courtyard at a more oblique angle than they do in more southerly latitudes.

(opposite) The forecourt of the Humble Administrator's Garden in Suzhou, China, is a prelude to one of the foremost gardens in China. The entire garden complex, built in 1509 by retired Imperial Inspector Wang Xian Chen, comprises over twelve acres of poetically juxtaposed landscapes and pavilions. The garden's design and its name stem from an essay penned by the Jin writer Pan Yue titled "Staying at Home Idle," which extols the humble virtues of tending and selling a vegetable crop.

According to a plaque at the entrance, the garden complex was "donated" to the Chinese people in the early 1950s in the aftermath of the revolution. UNESCO declared the Humble Administrator's Garden a World Heritage Site in 1997. © Arrol Gellner

often multistoried arcades, which provided a sheltered way to pass between buildings without having to go into the outside world.

SPANISH COURTYARDS

By far, the European country with the richest courtyard history is Spain. A staple of Spanish architecture for centuries, partly due to Spain's mild climate, the courtyard allowed for easy indoor-outdoor living. Of all the regions of Spain, Andalusia (*Andalucía* in Spanish) is best known for courtyard-inspired architecture. One of the most beautiful courtyard complexes in Andalusia is the Alhambra in the city of Granada. The famed beauty of the Alhambra is celebrated in postcards, books, and literature. Poet Francisco de Icaza (1863–1925) best described the glory of the Alhambra in this verse:

> *Dale limosna, mujer*
> *que no hay en la vida nada*
> *como la pena de ser*
> *ciego en Granada.*

> *Give him some money, woman,*
> *because there is nothing*
> *like the pity of being*
> *blind in Granada.*

The Alhambra was built over a period of many years, beginning with the construction of the Alcazaba by Mohammed V in 1238. Most of the major elements were completed by 1354, but additions, modifications, and reconstructions went on for centuries.

The courtyard of San Lorenzo (above and facing), the parish church of the Medici family, is a perfect example of a cloister garden. The courtyard is planted with orange trees, boxwood hedges, and pomegranate trees. Construction of the cloister, designed by Filippo Brunelleschi, began in 1420. Architecturally, it is comprised of a double tier of Ionic columns; the bottom row ringing the loggia supports graceful arches, while the top row supports the roof.

On the Isle of Iona, just off the coast of Scotland, is one of the most lovingly restored cloisters in the world at Iona Abbey, which traces its roots to AD 563 when St. Columbia arrived on Iona and established a monastery. Significant building took place in the late 1400s, but the abbey fell into disrepair after the Reformation in the 1560s. Preliminary restoration work began on the abbey grounds in 1874; restoration of the abbey began in 1902 and continues to this day under the supervision of the Iona Community, a religious organization that works for social and political change. The reconstruction of the cloisters is the most striking aspect of the restoration, since cloisters of this type are rare in Scotland. The stunning modern carvings on the column capitals depict Scottish flora and fauna. At the center of the cloister is a modern sculpture, The Descent of the Spirit, created by Lithuanian sculptor Jacques Lipchitz.

(opposite) Detail of the column capitals, which illustrate the local flora and fauna.

THE COURTYARD COMES TO AMERICA

Early forts, which possessed all the architectural elements of a courtyard, developed around frontier outposts and in conjunction with Spanish missions in the West. But true residential courtyards, which are urban in nature, didn't become a part of the architectural canvas of America until towns and cities developed. The first courtyards and courtyard gardens on the East Coast were, understandably, developed around English garden principles. Re-created examples can be seen today in Colonial Williamsburg, Virginia. Most of the garden courtyards in private homes had a well at the center with planting beds radiating outward. These courtyards are fine examples of English garden design with a symmetric and rigid layout, precisely clipped hedges, and geometric parterres (ornamental gardens). Courtyards on the East Coast and in the Midwest never became a large part of the residential architectural vocabulary. Relatively abundant land and correspondingly large lots combined with a ready water supply made sweeping lawns the staple and the home-owner's preference in landscaping. But two other regions of America would embrace the courtyard with gusto.

In California and the Southwest, Spanish missionaries built a string of missions beginning with Mission San Diego de Acala in 1769. These missions hosted America's first large-scale courtyards. Although one thinks of missions as exclusively religious structures, they actually served as agricultural, religious, and protective structures for their communities. Their courtyards were used as corrals, courtyard perimeters served as barracks and prison rooms, and only a small part of the mission housed a chapel. One need look no further than the Alamo to see the multiple uses of a mission courtyard. That famed mission was a fortification, corral, and chapel. But before the Spanish-inspired and court-yard-themed architecture could get much of a foothold, easterners in search of gold brought their own brand of architecture to the West.

One of the more interesting European-style cloisters isn't found in Europe. Perched high upon a hill in Fort Tryon Park on the fringes of New York City, The Cloisters is a complex of medieval buildings containing medieval art and courtyards. Completed in 1938 with funds provided by John D. Rockefeller Jr., the elements of The Cloisters were assembled from bits and pieces of cloisters in Europe that were disassembled and shipped to America.

This photograph depicts the Cuxa Cloister, assembled from pieces of the cloister of the Benedictine monastery Saint-Michel-de-Cuxa in the Pyrenees Mountains on the border of France and Spain. The monastery was constructed between 1130 and 1146, sacked in the seventeenth century, and fell into disrepair by the nineteenth century. The reconstruction of the Cuxa Cloister is about half of the original 156-by-128-foot size. Portions of stonework had to be refabricated, so new stone was cut from the original twelfth-century quarry in France. The octagonal fountain that sits at the center of the cloister is from the nearby thirteenth-century monastery of Saint-Génis-des-Fontaines.

All of the column capitals in these photographs come from the original abbey church of Saint-Michel-de-Cuxa. The deeply carved capitals depict a number of delightful assemblages of flora and fauna, including acanthus leaves, monkeys in a variety of poses, demons clutching eagles by the neck, and crouching lions.

So, rather than developing into a dominant architectural style, the missions and their courtyards languished for decades.

Fortunately, the mission styles were rediscovered in the waning years of the nineteenth century, thanks in large part to the efforts of an organization called the Association for the Preservation of the Missions, and a handful of noted architects, including A. Page Brown and Julia Morgan. Because of their efforts, the mission style was resurrected and given a new name—Mission Revival. But it would take a war and an exhibition in San Diego to fully launch the courtyard as a part of America's architectural vocabulary.

A GRAND EXPOSITION AND A GREAT WAR

In 1915, the Panama Canal was completed after seven tortuous years of effort. A great celebration was planned in San Diego, the closest American port to the canal. The task of designing the buildings for the San Diego-Panama-California Exposition fell upon architect Bertram Goodhue, who drew his inspiration from the Spanish Baroque architecture of the late seventeenth and early eighteenth century. San Diegans were so taken with Goodhue's clay-tiled courtyards, bubbling fountains, and shady arcades that his creations, made of the less-than-permanent

The Bonnefont Cloister is largely a re-creation based on a detailed 1807 survey of the cloister at Cistercian abbey at Bonnefont-en-Comminges southwest of Toulouse in southern France. Built in the late thirteenth or early fourteenth century, the abbey was actually founded in 1136. By the middle of the nineteenth century, pieces of the abbey had been scattered about the local countryside and incorporated into a number of other buildings. As seen in The Cloisters in New York, the Bonnefont Cloister retains only two of its original four covered walkways, but keeps the 109-by-78-foot size described in an 1807 survey. Many of the plants and trees in the cloister garden were named on a list that Charlemagne proscribed for the imperial gardens at Aachen, Germany.

(opposite) The Trie Cloister incorporates carved marble architectural elements salvaged from the late-fifteenth-century Carmelite convent at Trie-en-Bigorre in the Pyrenees, the monastery at Larreule, and possibly the abbey of Saint-Sever-de-Rustan, as well as modern re-creations. The column capitals represent biblical scenes such as the Creation and Abraham sacrificing Isaac, among others. The lime-stone cross topping the fountain at the center of the cloister is a composite of late-sixteenth- and early-seventeenth-century elements found in the Vosges region of northeast France. The lower element shows carvings of seven of the apostles and John the Baptist. Mounted directly on the cross are two sculptures, one of Saint Anne holding the Christ Child and the other of two saints.

Swiss-born architect Josias Joesler designed the arcaded courtyard of St. Philips in the Hill Episcopal Church in Tucson, Arizona. Joesler's creation, which was constructed in 1936, is reminiscent of eighteenth-century mission churches in California and the Southwest and is among the architect's finest works. The courtyard contains a small pool, with tile pathways that connect the arcades. Much of the timeless beauty of the Spanish Revival style comes from its simple palette of materials: clay, wood, and cement.

materials of lath and plaster, were ultimately recast in more durable materials.

Meanwhile, America entered World War I in Europe and sent troops overseas, giving many young men their first experience with another culture. After the war, some of those who entered the building trades incorporated parts of the designs they saw in Europe into their work. The most interesting style that emerged from their remembrances of Europe was the Storybook style, which echoed the high-pitched roofs and stucco exteriors of rural European homes. In the European cities, the soldiers often found clusters of houses grouped around a central courtyard, something virtually unknown in America.

Spain's entire Andalusia region has always been a prime destination for students of architecture. During World War I, when much of Europe was a battlefield, architecture students couldn't visit many traditional European locations. Therefore, the war-free Iberian Peninsula, which did not play a major role in the war, became a popular travel alternative for tourists and students. In Spain, particularly in the Andalusia region, they encountered a type of architecture similar to the missions in California and the Southwest, but much more irregular, fluid, and modestly proportioned. There was also one feature different from almost anything in America: courtyards. The Andalusian architecture fired the American students with ideas, and thanks to a huge building boom in Southern California, young architects were able to apply their ideas almost immediately after their return to the States. Thus, the battlefields of Europe helped bring Spanish architecture, Storybook architecture, and courtyards to another continent.

COURTYARD HOUSING

The first adaptations of the Andalusian-style courtyards were seen in apartment courts in Los Angeles, developed in the 1920s. This style was perfectly suited to the mild Southern California climate and readily embraced by Angelenos, particularly those employed in the transitory film industry. The modest size of the apartments were greatly expanded by the courtyard and seemed ideal for the private yet outdoor lifestyle desired by the film industry community. Decades later, courtyard apartments are still very much in demand by Angelenos, and what was a relatively inexpensive dwelling in the 1920s has become a pricey address in the twenty-first century.

Arriving about the same time as the apartment courts were bungalow courts, which represented a more open style of courtyard housing. These tidy courts, comprised of small freestanding cottages arranged around an open area for all to enjoy, were marketed to singles and young married couples. Usually constructed along streetcar lines, bungalow courts encouraged the use of public transportation, with automobiles usually confined to alleys surrounding the court or to a separate parking area. Eventually, some of the bungalow courts evolved into accommodations for transitory visitors. Dubbed "motor-hotels," they were the precursors of our modern motels.

After languishing for years, bungalow courts are back in style as part of the New Urbanism movement that emerged in the 1990s. Looking to be closer to the activity and energy of the city, young professionals are restoring old homes and reclaiming deteriorating neighborhoods. Not all of those interested in moving to the city want to restore an old house, so savvy contractors are building new

(top) Most early large-scale courtyards were rather spartan affairs. Their main purposes were used for protection, for convenient egress between buildings, as a place for markets, and as a place to corral animals. The Cour d'Honneur (Court of Honor) in Paris, is still used for military parades, and part of the huge Hotel des Invalides complex, built from 1671 to 1676 by Louis XIV, is certainly a courte a la carte. Nothing, not even a pattern, breaks up the huge parade grounds. A keen observer can spy Emil Seurre's statue of the Little Corporal (Napoleon) on the second level, observing the grounds for all eternity.

(bottom) Add a few benches, a fountain, shrubbery, and some flowers, and the formerly utilitarian courtyard becomes a courtyard garden—a place to sit and enjoy nature and the outdoors. This court-yard garden is part of a complex of buildings built for the 1915 Panama-California Exposition in San Diego. The exposition was so popular with San Diegans that most of the temporary buildings, originally built of lath and plaster, were rebuilt with more permanent materials. Their cool colonnades, sheltered courtyards, and well-kept gardens are now part of Balboa Park.

In a courtyard near the Pantheon in Rome, the surface of the courtyard sprouts some greenery. Diagonal cobblestone pathways direct walkers from building to building without treading on the grass. Despite the greenery, the courtyard does not invite people to linger, as there are no chairs, benches, or even a fountain to gather around. The courtyard merely provides a pleasant place to walk through, not a place to spend time.

One of the six courtyards in the Neues Rathaus (New Town Hall) in Munich, Germany. An orderly geometric pattern breaks up the surface of the courtyard, providing a foil for the complex ornamentation on the buildings. The Neues Rathaus was built from 1867 to 1919 in a pseudo-Netherlands Gothic style. Perhaps the best example of the pseudo-historical style is Neuschwanstein Castle in the Bavarian Alps, commissioned to be built between 1869 and 1886 by King Ludwig II, also known as the Mad King of Bavaria. This magnificent castle was the inspiration for the Fantasyland castle at Disneyland.

bungalow courts to fulfill the needs of those wanting to live in a tidy, secure urban home. This phenomenon, for the most part, has been limited to the West Coast, but there have been pockets of activity elsewhere. Whether the trend gains widespread acceptance throughout the country remains to be seen.

NEW ORLEANS

The other American region closely associated with courtyards is the city of New Orleans, especially in the French Quarter (Vieux Carre). Although courtyards by their nature are secluded, private, and inaccessible to the general public, visitors to New Orleans can experience their ambiance as many private courtyards have been converted into commercial spaces.

The earliest homes in New Orleans, built during the French period, were wide and spacious and often contained a small garden. Unfortunately, two disastrous fires in the late eighteenth century essentially leveled the town. Afterwards, new homes were built right up to the street on smaller lots that were long and narrow, resulting in a minimal front yard and large walled courtyards in the back. These early courtyards acted as utility areas, with a kitchen usually at the center or off to one side. The rear of the courtyard was reserved for poultry and a privy, and the rest of the courtyard served as a laundry and multiuse area.

Usually the courtyards were paved and had a drainage gully to channel off excess water. If there was a garden, it was customarily quite minimal since most produce was procured at nearby public markets. Flowers, shrubs, and other ornamental features usually remained an afterthought. With the advent of indoor plumbing, electricity, and air-conditioning, the kitchen, bathroom, and laundry were moved indoors. Thus, for a period of time in the late nineteenth and early twentieth centuries, New Orleans courtyards fell into disuse and disrepair and became little more than storage areas. But the establishment of a French Quarter preservation society at the beginning of the twentieth century led to increased tourism and property values, and gave new life to the rundown courtyards. New Orleans courtyards were resurrected and transformed from spartan utility areas to lush retreats during the 1920s and 1930s. This well-documented transformation was celebrated with gloriously colored postcards. Nowadays, many of the French Quarter's courtyards have been converted to lush restaurants and bars that offer a cool and shady respite from the noisy, sweltering streets.

NEW CONSTRUCTIONS

Since courtyards are an architectural feature of a home, they must be built into the overall home design when the home is constructed. In today's society, many homeowners are looking for ways to add a courtyard-like space to their decidedly un-courtyard-like home. Creative builders, landscape architects, and the homeowners themselves are figuring out ways to turn ordinary lawns, front yards, backyards, and side yards into lush Edens. This phenomenon is often seen in, but not limited to, those climates with a well-established indoor-outdoor lifestyle. These new courtyard-like spaces are emerging as outdoor rooms. Some are diminutive—used as quiet meditative areas—while others sport swimming pools, full kitchens, and patios large enough for dancing. Whatever the use, realtors say courtyards are often at the top of a homebuyer's wish list. Small, medium, or large, courtyards serve the purpose of providing a private space away from the noise, congestion, and stress of modern urban life.

Certainly the Piazza San Pietro (St. Peter's Square) at the Vatican stretches the definition of a courtyard, but since it has two fountains and is almost completely surrounded by a protective wall of buildings, it fits within the broad description of a courtyard. The Piazza San Pietro outgrows the definition of a courtyard because of its size, not its configuration. The plaza is in the shape of an enormous ellipse and measures over 300 yards at its largest dimension. Designed by Gian Lorenzo Bernini, the area symbolizes St. Peter embracing the world—St. Peter's Basilica represents his head and the two colonnades with massive 60-foot Doric columns represent his arms. At the center of the ellipse and flanked by two fountains is an 83-foot-tall Egyptian obelisk originally brought to Rome in AD 38 by Caligula, and placed in its present location in 1576.

(opposite) One of the most majestic castle courtyards is the courtyard of Heidelberg Castle in Germany. The construction of the castle took over 400 years, starting with the residence of Prince Elector Ruprecht III in the fifteenth century. On the left is the Friedrich's Building, built by Friedrich IV, who ruled from 1583 to 1610. On the right is the Ottheinrich Building, constructed in early German Renaissance style during the rule of the Elector Ottheinrich, who ruled from 1556 to 1559. Sandwiched between the two buildings is the Hall of Mirrors, built during the reign of Friedrich II (1544–1556). Today, besides being the passageway between buildings at Heidelberg Castle, the courtyard is a venue for summer concerts.

Another courtyard-like plaza completely surrounded by buildings is the Poble Espanyol (Spanish Town), in Barcelona, Spain, constructed in 1929 for the International Exposition. The complex consists of 116 buildings that represent all of the regions and architectural styles of Spain. Poble Espanyol was renovated in the 1980s as part of a citywide sprucing up in preparation for the Barcelona 1992 Olympics. The courtyard also serves as a large open-air venue for concerts and theater productions. Winding streets lead off the main courtyard to artisans' shops many with small courtyards of their own.

The center of focus in the House of Hospitality's courtyard in San Diego's Balboa Park is Woman of Tehuantepec, a sculpture of a seated Indian woman, executed by artist Donal Hord. The House of Hospitality was one of the many buildings constructed for the 1915–16 Panama-California Exposition, a celebration of San Diego and the completion of the Panama Canal. The sculpture was added during the remodeling of the House of Hospitality, with work done under the direction of noted architect Richard Requa for the 1935–36 California-Pacific International Exposition. The entire two-story structure was razed in 1995 due to structural problems, but was faithfully reconstructed and reopened in 1997. The spacious courtyard is a true courtyard, since it has a water element and is completely surrounded by habitable spaces.

The courtyard of the Southern California Counties Building was one of the many court-yards at the Panama-California Exposition, and for many people, this was their first experience with a court-yard. The exposition set the stage for Spanish Colonial Revival architecture, a style that still remains popular almost a century later.

The Andalusian architecture of Spain is wonderfully interpreted in the courtyard of the Broadway Village shopping center in Tucson, Arizona. Designed in 1939 by architect Josias Joesler, the courtyard and surrounding buildings are a veritable encyclopedia of patterns, forms, color palettes, and textures. These seemingly diverse elements all work together under the umbrella of the Spanish Revival style. Shopping center developers have rediscovered the concept of using a variety of visual elements as they seek antidotes to the sameness of post–World War II shopping center design.

(opposite) Renowned architect Addison Mizner designed the courtyard of Via Parigi in Palm Beach, Florida, in 1925. Mizner got his start in Florida in 1919 when he designed the Everglades Club by superbly blending Spanish Colonial Revival, Andalusian, and Italianate styles on a tract of land formerly known as Joe's Alligator Farm.

The center of focus at Via Parigi is the octagonal fountain made of coquina stone, a native Florida limestone containing fossil shells and corals. The meandering walkways and casually disposed facades suggest random growth and provide an ever-changing vista for pedestrians. Note the projecting balcony of pecky cypress, a species of timber considered worthless before Mizner began featuring it in his work.

The main elements of this unique Storybook-style courtyard in Los Angeles known as The Grove were moved here from another location. The original courtyard and cottages were designed by architect Allen Siple in 1932; Elda Muir made additions in 1940. When a major construction project threatened the destruction of the complex, the project's developers moved the buildings to this location off Wilshire Boulevard in 1988, where they were reconfigured for office use. Despite the move, most of the complex survived intact, with some parts reconstructed. Elements of Storybook-style architecture can be seen in the diminutive scale of the cottages, random paving pattern, casual layout of the buildings, artificial aging, and use of one material to suggest another, such as the "log" posts of the wishing well that are actually reinforced colored concrete.

COURTYARD AND PRISON ROOMS IN THE CABILDO
NEW ORLEANS, LA.— 151

Because of their walled construction, courtyards also worked quite well for corralling disreputable characters. This post-card view aptly illustrates the utilitarian use and stark appearance of courtyards in New Orleans' French Quarter. A common feature to all French Quarter courtyards was a drainage gutter, visible at the center of the illustration. It was not until the twentieth century that those courtyards would be used for more pleasurable activities.

Little has changed architecturally at Pat O'Brien's Bar in New Orleans since the 1940s when the post-card view on the right was taken. Before O'Brien purchased the building in 1942, the site, which was first developed in 1791, housed the French Territory's first Spanish theater. The entrance to Pat O'Brien's is through an old carriageway, which also served as the entrance to the theater. After passing the main bar and the piano bar, the carriageway opens to a 4,000-square-foot courtyard. Pat O'Brien's simple motto is "have fun," and that is precisely what patrons have been doing for decades. A relaxing atmosphere is aided by generous servings of O'Brien's intoxicating signature libation, the Hurricane (more than one million served). The courtyard is landscaped with trees and plants native to Louisiana.

French Quarter Courtyard of the Two Sisters, Royal Street, New Orleans, La.

35

One of New Orleans' most noted dining establishments is the Court of the Two Sisters at 613 Royal Street. The court's history goes back to the 1700s when Royal Street was known as Governor's Row, since it was home to five governors, two state supreme court justices, one future justice of the United States Supreme court, and a future president of the United States. The court acquired its modern name when Erma and Bertha Camors, two sisters from an aristocratic Creole family, opened a notions store in the late nineteenth century. The sisters catered to stylish New Orleanian women and outfitted them with formal gowns, lace, and perfumes imported from Paris. After the sisters' death within two months of each other in 1944, the property underwent a succession of owners before it was turned into a restaurant. The owners claim that the Court of the Two Sisters is the largest courtyard in the French Quarter.

Ultimately, courtyards are intimate and peaceful outdoor rooms where one is encouraged to linger. That sentiment is aptly illustrated by Dorothy Frances Gurney's (1858–1932) poem Garden Thoughts:

> The kiss of the sun for pardon,
> The song of the birds for mirth,
> One is nearer God's heart in a garden
> Than anywhere else on earth.

According to scholars, the word court *was first used in the English language in 1175. It probably was derived from the Latin word* cortem *(enclosed yard) as well as from* curia *(sovereign's assembly). Most legal assemblies were overseen by a member of royalty; thus by 1292,* court *became associated with justice. By 1493, the venues for legal proceedings became known as courthouses.*

The Pima County Courthouse in Tucson, Arizona, pictured above left is one of very few courthouses that has a real courtyard. Designed in 1928 by Roy Place, the courthouse is predominantly Spanish Colonial Revival architecture, with some Southwest and Moorish embellishments. Some notable features are the dazzlingly colored tile dome, the Churrigueresque embellishments surrounding the passage and entryways (first seen in America at the 1919 Panama-California Exposition in San Diego), and the beautiful tile fountain. In 1978, fifty years after it was built, the Pima County Courthouse was placed on the National Register of Historic Places.

OLD SPANISH COURTYARD,
NEW ORLEANS, LA.—39

COURTYARD OF LITTLE THEATRE,
NEW ORLEANS, LA.—176

Bosque Court
in the Vieux Carré
New Orleans, La.

OLD COURTYARD, FRENCH QUARTER,
NEW ORLEANS, LA.—17

Courtyard, Governor Claiborne Home,
New Orleans, La.

Fan Window in Governor Claiborne Home,
New Orleans, La.

COURTYARD, LITTLE THEATRE,
NEW ORLEANS, LA.

Brulatour Courtyard, 520 Royal Street
New Orleans, La.   19

community
COURTYARDS

Some of the most interesting and accessible courtyards are located in group housing complexes known as courts, which are primarily an urban phenomenon. They were created when little clusters of cottages were grouped around a central courtyard. They were usually built adjacent to streetcar lines or on major thoroughfares, since they were intended for single people or young married couples who commuted to jobs on public transportation. Bungalow courts and cottage courts are detached single-story structures, grouped around a central courtyard. Often there was a related two-story structure usually occupied by the property owner or manager. Generally, bungalow courts were built in the Arts and Crafts style, while cottage courts were built in a variety of styles. Apartment courts, like bungalow and cottage courts, are grouped around a central courtyard, but apartment courts do not have detached units.

Most of these courts were developed in the early part of the twentieth century. Along with auto and trailer camps, they became the template for motor hotels (motels). The new urbanism movement that began in the late twentieth century has brought about a revival of residential courts. Most of these modern courts are located in the more temperate West Coast of the United States, which has a long tradition of the indoor-outdoor lifestyle.

Many public buildings incorporate atriums, making them the easiest public courtyards to see. An atrium has the form of a courtyard with one major exception: the glass roof. Because of their all-weather aspect, atriums can be seen in all regions of the United States. Atriums can also run the entire length of a building, and it is here that they break out of the courtyard mold. Well-designed atriums provide a respite for weary tourists in museums and for haggard shoppers in malls.

The Reinway court, built in 1916 in Pasadena, California, is a classic example of a bungalow court. The owner's two-story residence can be seen in the rear. Now, almost a century later and 500 miles north, the Reinway has been reborn as the Doe Mill Court in Chico, California. The Doe Mill Court retains many of the elements of Reinway court, including the detached bungalows, and pergola-style entrance.

BOWEN COURT, PASADENA, CAL. 34 Bungalows furnished and unfurnished.

In the early twentieth century, postcards depicting bucolic courtyards attracted thousands of people to southern California. Bungalow courts were especially attractive to single people and young married couples.

(opposite top) The Reinway Court, built in 1916 in Pasadena, California, is a classic example of a bungalow court. The owner's two-story residence can be seen in the rear.

(opposite) Now, almost a century later and 500 miles north, the Reinway has been reborn as the Doe Mill Court in Chico, California. The Doe Mill Court retains many of the elements of Reinway Court, including the detached bungalows, and pergola-style entrance.

A brick-paved parking area serves as an intermediate space between the street and the courtyard. After passing through iron gates, visitors are greeted by a verdant paradise whose center of focus is a star-shaped fountain enclosed by a fanciful quatrefoil. The courtyard hosts an enviable collection of plants, including well-tended hedges, bamboo, palm trees, a bright, mature bougainvillaea, and a variety of roses providing splashes of color. The Andalusian-inspired architecture, with its compact scale and delicate lines, is a perfect foil for the delightful courtyard garden.

(opposite) It's hard to imagine a more appealing courtyard than the Andalusia in Hollywood, California. Tinseltown heartthrobs, such as Clara Bow, Cesar Romero, and Clint Eastwood, have all lived here. Arthur and Nina Zwebell, a well-to-do couple from the Midwest who moved to Los Angeles in 1921, built the Andalusia in 1926. From 1923 until 1928, the Zwebells built half a dozen stunning courtyard apartments in Hollywood. Of all their creations (Villa Primavera, Patio del Moro, La Ronda, Andalusia, El Cabrillo and Casa Laguna), the Andalusia is unquestionably their greatest achievement.

(above left) A horseshoe arch straight out of the architectural palette of North Africa and the Middle East frames an imposing door that leads to the Patio del Moro in Hollywood. Designed in 1925 by Arthur and Nina Zwebell, it appears that the Patio del Moro was constructed by builders versant in the Storybook style, a type of pseudo-historic architecture developed in Los Angeles in the early 1920s. The Storybook style uses special techniques to suggest artificial aging. In order to make Patio del Moro look centuries old, the builder made the door out of unfinished planks with iron studs, used flat Roman bricks in a slightly irregular pattern, and painted the rough stucco wall in a faux finish.

(above right) The fireplace at Patio del Moro is centrally located on a wall between two apartments. Despite Southern California's reputation for year-round warm weather, summer evenings can be quite cool. The fireplace takes the chill out of the air and becomes a gathering spot because of its convenient location.

(opposite) Through another horseshoe arch at Patio del Moro, the visitor enters into the lush courtyard. The courtyard floor, set with bricks in a basket-weave pattern, is almost completely shaded by a host of tropical plants, including mature bamboo and a banana tree that produces petite bananas. An outdoor fireplace is just to the left of a square-paneled door that leads to one of seven apartments.

The Villa Primavera is the earliest known surviving example of the courts designed by Arthur and Nina Zwebell. The Spanish-style apartments built of wood and stucco completely surround the square court-yard, and all ten apartments can be accessed by it. In Los Angeles, where the automobile is an essential part of life, it is a challenge to integrate sufficient parking spaces into courts without overwhelming the architecture. The Zwebells solved the problem by putting all of the parking in one space (off to the right in the photograph). Thus the parking spaces are hidden by a low wall and are out of sight if not out of mind.

(left) This imposing outdoor fireplace occupies one side of the Villa Primavera's courtyard; above its firebox, a swelling stucco hood is surmounted by a cast-stone relief of the Madonna and Child. A pair of wrought-iron sconces hangs on either side. The chimney cap, with its grillwork of diagonal clay tiles, is a typical Andalusian detail frequently seen in Spanish Revival work of the area.

(below) Casa Laguna, built in 1928, was the last of the Zwebells' courtyard projects. Twelve units surround the lush courtyard, complete with two of the Zwebells' trademark details: an outdoor fireplace located behind the palm tree's trunk on the right and a hand-painted tile fountain. The architectural style and layout—a two-story square box with rather straight lines—is similar to the Zwebells' first project, Villa Primavera. Seven round columns with diminutive Ionic capitals comprise the two-story loggia. They support a heavy beam, above which is a balcony with delicately carved balusters.

The El Cordova courtyard apartments in Long Beach, California, are a delightful potpourri of undulating architectural embellishments. El Cordova, now known as Rose Towers, is the best example of the collaboration between architect George D. Riddle and Monarch Construction. Built in 1928 during Long Beach's building boom, these apartments with their U-shaped courtyard are some of the most desirable in the community.

Close inspection of Rose Towers' courtyard apartments reveals a masterpiece of orchestrated chaos. Straight lines are amazingly elusive. Pathways that ought to be straight undulate their way through the courtyard. Delightfully chaotic features include pathways scored with random curves, exterior stairways peppered with hand-painted tiles, numerous balconies of wood or wrought iron, projecting bays, and openings comprised of round, pointed, and parabolic arches.

(facing) The builders placed the garages beneath the rear of the courtyard apartment buildings to relieve the main entrance from automobile traffic. This also gave them an opportunity to add interesting changes of level. At El Cordova, Riddle designed a twin set of stairs with stepped balustrades leading up to the patio above the garage; between them sits a wall fountain and pool that provides the focal point of El Cordova's courtyard landscaping.

The random brick pattern on the ground, steps formed to look like millions of visitors have trodden on them, multipaned windows, and a faux distressed finish all work together to suggest great age. The inner courtyard of Normandy Village looks like it belongs in rural France rather than next to the bustling campus of the University of California–Berkeley. The garden, visible through the passageway, is easily accessed via the courtyard and most of the eight unique apartments.

(opposite) A few years after architect William R. Yelland returned from his stint in France during World War I, he created one of America's most outstanding examples of Storybook-style architecture. From 1926 to 1928, Yelland built Normandy Village, an eight-unit apartment house, for his friend and fellow veteran Colonel Jack W. Thornburg. The architectural style suggests the places they had seen while serving in rural northern France. No detail was too small to escape Yelland's attention, from the swayed roof that imitates the effect of settling over time and the exaggerated, almost cartoonish stonework, to the frescoes high on the eaves and the ancient-looking lantern. Passing through the portal and entering the courtyard is like going back centuries in time.

Storybook-style architecture was developed in Los Angeles after the First World War. Some of the young men who served in the war moved to Los Angeles and took jobs building sets in the movie industry. At the time, the period film was the rage. Rudolph Valentino charmed women in The Sheik; *Errol Flynn swashbuckled through the seven seas, and Greta Garbo vamped her way around the world. Some of the set builders moonlighted building homes, and before long they were building some of those homes using techniques acquired while building sets for period films. However, before the Storybook style had a chance to spread much beyond California, the Great Depression arrived and pushed all things fun and expensive to the back burner. Good, intact examples of Storybook architecture are quite rare; thus, Normandy Village is a treasure.*

An arch made out of Carmel chalkstone forms the entrance to Stonehenge, a magical court in Alameda, California. This highly original cottage court was designed in 1926 and built from 1927 to 1929 by a man with an equally original name, Christopher Columbus Howard. The court's basic layout is essentially the same as a bungalow court, but the artificial aging of the cottages as well as the curving paths and the effervescent plantings exude a special charm seen only in whimsical Storybook-style architecture.

(opposite) Automobiles are relegated to a narrow alley in back of the cottages so there are no visual clues to remind residents they are living in a busy urban area. At the center of the courtyard amidst well-tended plantings is a moss-covered bubbling fountain complete with its own street lamp.

The West Building of the National Gallery of Art in Washington, D.C., contains two sumptuous courtyards that offer a pleasant respite for weary tourists. When it opened in 1941, the building and its courtyards was the largest marble structure in the world. A joint resolution of Congress created the building, which was constructed from 1937 to 1941 from plans by famed Beaux-Arts–trained architect John Russell Pope. Both courtyards are virtually identical except for their fountains and seasonal plantings. The West courtyard (opposite) contains a sculpture by French artist Jean-Baptiste Tuby I (1635-1700) titled Cherubs Playing with a Swan, created between 1672 and 1673. The East courtyard (left) contains a sculpture titled Cherubs Playing with a Lyre, created at the same time by French artist Pierre Legros I (1629-1714). Each courtyard is 106 by 76 feet, with walls and columns made of Indiana Shawnee limestone. The colonnades are composed of sixteen monolithic columns, each 24 feet high and 3-$\frac{1}{2}$ feet in diameter.

The sculpture Cherubs Playing with a Lyre sits on a stone pedestal. It was originally gilded in gold, and some traces can be seen under the wings.

Some of the most used and appreciated courtyards reside in public buildings, and few are appreciated more than courtyards incorporated into hospital designs. Tabitha Home in Lincoln, Nebraska, was originally built as an orphanage in 1890. Over the years, a series of additions and remodels expanded Tabitha's services to include rehabilitation, long-term care, and hospice care. A 28-by-36-foot courtyard that was part of a 1968 remodel of the nursing and rehabilitation center offers a pleasant oasis of trickling water and greenery amidst sterile hospital walls. The courtyard gives patients, staff, and visitors a place to be outdoors while staying safe and secure within the confines of the building.

(opposite) Four identical 101-by-87-foot courtyards are symmetrically arranged around the 400-foot central tower of the Nebraska State Capitol Building in Lincoln. Placed at the northeast, northwest, southeast and southwest corners of the building, the courtyards are completely surrounded by offices. The main floor of the capitol building is actually the second floor, while the first floor, which houses the offices and access to the courtyards, has the feel of a basement. Thanks to the light coming in through the windows from the courtyards, occupants of the first floor offices are spared a gloomy existence. The capitol building, built between 1922 and 1932, was designed by noted architect Bertram Goodhue, who designed the buildings and courtyards of the Panama-California Exposition in San Diego in 1915.

CHAPTER 2

COURTYARDS IN HISTORIC RESIDENTIAL ARCHITECTURE

Since America was first settled, court-yards have been a staple of vernacular American architecture. English-, French-, and Spanish-influenced courtyards, all with their unique aspects, were built in different regions of the country. The first courtyards constructed in the colonies used English garden landscape architecture as their template. At almost the same time, but on the other side of the continent, Spanish-style courtyards emerged in conjunction with California missions. By the beginning of the nineteenth century, the French-influenced Creole courtyard emerged in New Orleans after a series of disastrous fires in the late 1700s wiped out most of the original homes, which did not usually have courtyards.

But courtyards were hardly commonplace and were little more than a local curiosity. They did not truly come into their own until the early twentieth century with the emergence of the bungalow. This housing style was an architectural expression of the indoor-outdoor lifestyle espoused in the Arts and Crafts movement. This philosophy advocated the use of natural materials in homes designed with open rooms and porches that provided lots of light and fresh air. This aesthetic provided a springboard to introduce courtyards into bungalow designs. Not limited to bungalows, courtyards were also soon embraced by builders of Storybook-style homes in the 1920s and Spanish-style homes that flourished in California and the Southwest. But after World War II, Americans flocked to the newly minted suburbs where a large lawn rather than a tidy courtyard became the most desirable landscape element. Courtyards would have to wait a few decades before working back into mainstream architecture. That moment came in the 1970s when new urban pioneers started returning to the city. These newcomers refurbished neglected courtyards, carved new ones out of utility areas, and rediscovered the joys of an indoor-outdoor lifestyle in an urban setting.

Formal English gardens are green, intricate, and tidy. Their manicured hedges and lovely pathways evoke images of Alice scampering through the mazes of Wonderland. The focus of this 25-foot-square courtyard in San Francisco is a knot garden comprised of a boxwood hedge framed by thirteen Pittosporum undulatum *trees. Usually grown as a hedge, this tree is native to Tasmania and Queensland, Australia. Its fragrant flowers give the plant one of its common names, mock orange.*

The focal point of Colonial Williamsburg is the Governor's Palace and its surrounding gardens, built in stages during the early eighteenth century. The establishment and development of the gardens is largely due to Lieutenant Governor Alexander Spotswood, who served as governor of Virginia from 1710 to 1722. Upon his arrival in 1710, Spotswood proceeded to devote much of his time to establishing elaborate gardens designed in the formal English tradition. Hallmarks of Spotswood's English garden design at Colonial Williamsburg are symmetric and rigid layouts, precisely clipped hedges, and geometric parterres (ornamental gardens).

The Holly Garden is a small courtyard inspired by the engravings of Johannes Kips, a Dutch artist who made extremely detailed engravings of English gardens. The parterres—which usually contain seasonal bulbs, American holly, and annuals—are bordered with English ivy. The walkways are paved in marl— a mixture of clay, limestone and shell fragments.

Some of the earliest courtyards in America were constructed in Williamsburg, Virginia, now known as Colonial Williamsburg, which is a reconstruction of the eighteenth-century city of Williamsburg, whose restoration was begun in the 1920s.

The courtyard of the Towers Bed and Breakfast in Milford, Delaware, is a study in relaxed formality. Victorian courtyards are usually quite formal and ordered, but the owners of The Towers made this courtyard a bit less formal by using flowing, organic designs. A brick patio surrounds a rectangular pond with a gently spraying fountain; airy wire furniture, wispy plantings, and a whimsical sculpture of a dancing child complete the scene. The Towers Bed and Breakfast was built in 1783 and remodeled in 1891 in the Steamboat Gothic style.

This circa-1908 postcard depicts the courtyard of the Cora Hollister house (no longer extant) in Hollywood, California, designed by renowned Arts and Crafts architects Charles and Henry Greene. The Arts and Crafts style is particularly suited to courtyards because of the indoor-outdoor living philosophy espoused by its adherents.

The courtyard of the Gingerbread Mansion Bed and Breakfast, in Ferndale, California, plays host to leisurely breakfasts and afternoon teas. The flowery cast-iron furniture is in the effervescent Victorian style, just like the gingerbread on the house. The garden is planted with lush hydrangeas, cosmos, gladiolas, daisies, roses, and a variety of potted annuals.

Most of San Francisco's multicolored Victorian homes are shoehorned into 25-foot lots, leaving little room for expansive gardens. However, the owner of this Italianate-style home, built in 1878, managed to tuck a small courtyard between the house and a fence that runs along the property line. True to the Victorian esthetic best characterized as the joy of excess, the tiny courtyard is jam-packed with personal treasures and flea market finds.

(opposite) This hidden courtyard in the French Quarter (Vieux Carre) is a classic New Orleans Creole-style courtyard with tropical plants and a burbling fountain. Although courtyards are associated with the Vieux Carre as much as are beignets and intoxicating libations, courtyard gardens are a relatively recent invention. The first courtyards appeared in the late eighteenth century behind homes built on long, narrow lots. These courtyards were little more than utility areas housing the cookhouse, well, privy, laundry, and sometimes a small garden. In the twentieth century, the advent of indoor plumbing, washing machines, and air-conditioning, which allowed for indoor cooking, moved these utilities out of the courtyard and freed up the space for more pleasurable uses.

This petite courtyard of the B&W Courtyards Bed and Breakfast is on a quiet side street just four blocks from the French Quarter in New Orleans. After entering through a porte cochere, the rustic simplicity of the courtyard comes into view. The courtyard's pond, walls, and patio are a gallery for the owners' treasures brought from their travels to foreign countries and local flea markets, including a porcelain frog from Mexico, porcelain fish from China, and blue porcelain balls from Bali. A geranium in full flower at the center, horsetails on the far right, ginger on the far left, and night-blooming jasmine at the center rear dominate the courtyard. The surrounding buildings are part of a Creole compound built in 1854 that consisted of a main house, outbuildings, and slave quarters.

(right, top) An irritated frog lounges in the pool while a blue-and-white frog climbs the wall (right, bottom).

The pond in the B&W Courtyards is simply constructed with a wood frame and a plastic pond liner. A fountain made by fitting a concrete urn with hoses and a pump provides the soothing sound of gently flowing water. The wooden wall holds the owner's collection of fish plates. An asparagus fern grows on the wall with African irises (right) and a blue yucca nearby. One of the most interesting elements of the courtyard is the paving material: what looks like Saltillo tile is actually painted concrete.

(above, and opposite bottom) A more open courtyard theme continues in the back garden. Holly ferns, azaleas, impatiens, and liriope provide a variety of cool colors and textures. Dominating the rear garden is a huge live oak tree, providing ample shade for everything nearby, including a beautiful sculpture made especially for the garden by noted local sculptor Enrique Alfarez.

(opposite, top) This majestic Venetian Gothic–style home, designed by architect Francis J. MacDonnell, sits near the campus of Tulane University in uptown New Orleans. The home, pleasantly situated on a key lot in a quiet cul-de-sac, appeared in the February 1910 issue of Architecture and Its Allies *magazine. The quiet location prompted the owners to install a courtyard in the front of the house. There are two other gardens, one on the side and one in back. The front courtyard was originally a simple grass plot bordered by an overgrown Pittosporum hedge and azalea beds. The current homeowner transformed the courtyard into a much more enjoyable brick parterre courtyard, centered on a round fishpond containing water lilies and papyrus. A small fountain adds the necessary water sounds.*

The vine-covered house forms the north wall of the courtyard; a stucco-and-iron fence, home to cascading Confederate jasmine, forms the west and south borders. Of particular note is the Romeo and Juliet balcony and Moorish/Venetian Gothic arches. A tall viburnum hedge forms the east perimeter. A pathway visible on the right leads through an iron archway to the less-formal side gardens of tall sweet olive trees, magnolias, sasanqua trees, and gardenias.

The courtyard parterres, set in geometric brick walkways and outlined in small trimmed boxwoods, each have a tree-form pink Indian Hawthorne in the center. Also in the parterres is white cyclamen. At other times of the year, Candidum caladiums and coral diascia thrive here.

Behind the fountain wall of this courtyard in New Orleans is a tall hedge of Eagleston holly. Framing the wall are twin duranta bushes trained as trees. Gardeners love duranta for its ability to attract butterflies, so it's a popular plant in Southern gardens. The centerpiece of the fountain is an antique urn that has been converted to a container and planted with cascading lantana and a witch hazel tree. Landscape architect Rene Fransen designed the fountain, herringbone paving, and the four garden beds that complete and frame the entire ensemble.

(opposite) The courtyard possesses the refinement and ambiance of the fine Southern home it adjoins. The two story house at the rear supports window boxes festooned with cascading white lantana, and trellises are laden with evergreen wisteria and Confederate jasmine. Wire baskets on the upper terrace of the house at the right are brimming with blue plumbago, and cascading lantana and white sasanqua under the windows anchor the base of the house. Two red Japanese maples frame the house, with one in the middle of the photograph and one on the far right. Boxwood topiary spheres punctuate the herringbone-patterned brick paving.

Venture around the back of this New Orleans house and you'll find an intimate secret garden tucked between the house and the rear garden wall. A greenhouse covered with ficus provides a third wall. At the center of the courtyard sits a fountain made from an antique urn, surrounded by four putti representing the four seasons. The fountain contains water hyacinths, pickerelweed, iris, and cyperus plants. In the beds around the fountain are butterfly iris, lamium, and garden violets. A sweet olive tree can be seen at the right rear, while sasanqua trees frame the entrance. Noted landscape designer Babie Hardie and architect Douglas Freret designed the secret garden.

(opposite) Noted Santa Barbara builder Joseph Plunkett designed the El Presidio Building in 1946. The El Presidio utilizes Andalusian-inspired architecture as do some of Plunkett's other public projects, most notably the Arlington Theater and the city's municipal airport. Plunkett used patinated surfaces to suggest great age, best expressed on El Presidio's clock tower. The building and courtyard serve a number of commercial offices.

Construction of La Casa de Estudillo (The Estudillo House) in the Old Town section of San Diego began in 1827. Casa Estudillo's builder, Capitan Jose Maria Estudillo, was a retired San Diego fort commander. His original plan called for an L-shaped building and was later modified to its present U shape. The house has two courtyards: the outer courtyard, which is more like a corral, and the inner courtyard pictured above. Much of the courtyard was reserved for growing flowers and edibles such as fruits, vegetables, herbs, and spices. The family maintained the Estudillo House until the 1880s, after which it fell into disrepair. In 1908, after going through a succession of owners, architect Hazel Waterman restored the Estudillo House, and it was rechristened Ramona's Marriage Place, based on Helen Hunt Jackson's popular novel Ramona. Thanks to some clever repackaging, including dozens of colored postcards (bottom left and right), the old casa sprang back to life and quickly became a popular place to get stylishly hitched. Ramona's Marriage Place operated until the early 1950s, and by the late 1960s it was part of the California State Park system.

The courtyard and the surrounding buildings of Rancho Los Alamitos (Ranch of the Little Cottonwoods) in Long Beach, California, span the Spanish Colonial period, Mexican Territorial period, and American era. Juan Nieto built the original four-room adobe house after his father's death in 1804. The courtyard was created by additions to the original home in 1842 by Don Abel Sterns and in 1925 by the Bixby family. In the early twentieth century, the courtyard and surrounding grounds were enhanced with extensively landscaped gardens. Today, it serves as a cool, quiet retreat.

One would be hard-pressed to find a more stunning example of a Spanish Colonial Revival courtyard than the tranquil one at La Casa Nueva in the City of Industry, California. Casa Nueva was built for Walter P. Temple and designed by the well-known Los Angeles firm of Walker and Eisen. Today La Casa Nueva is open to the public as part of the Workman and Temple Family Homestead Museum.

The orderly colonnade, peppered with container shrubbery, frames the tranquil courtyard. A fountain commands the central position, while a planter cleverly constructed of reproductions of the original cement-sheathed adobe millstones and planted with salvia provides a splash of color. The ground cover is ivy; a New Zealand flame tree rises well above the second story; and a carob tree frames the open southern end of the courtyard.

The millstones in the center of the fountain at La Casa Nueva, which date to the mid-nineteenth century, probably came from the gristmill operated by Walter Temple's grandfather, William Workman. The fountain and many other of the architectural elements of the house are examples of how Temple sought to integrate family history into the design of his home. The shrubs around the fountain are boxwood.

This courtyard in San Diego is behind a 1926 Spanish Colonial Revival house designed by renowned architect Richard S. Requa, who was so enamored with Spanish architecture that he wrote a book in 1929 titled Old World Inspiration for American Architecture. One of the chapters was devoted to courts and patios in the Mediterranean. In this home, found in the Kensington Heights area of San Diego, the transition from the indoors to the veranda to the courtyard is virtually seamless. Of particular interest are the heavy Moroccan-style curtains (in the center of the photograph, next to a bougainvillaea) that can be closed to block the sun, allowing the veranda to remain an integral part of the living space. The curtains, added by the homeowner, were a common device used often in 1920s Southern California architecture. Curtains of this type were adapted from designs seen in North Africa. Many homes in Southern California still have curtain rods on the outside of their windows, but homeowners are clueless as to why they are there.

(opposite) The ornamental pool, added by the current owner in 1983, is a fine example of how a relatively large architectural element can be integrated into a small space. The pool is elevated eighteen inches above the tiled surface, allowing for extra seating during parties. A variety of native plants surround the pool; because they are all in containers, they can be moved and rearranged with the seasons. The dominant color is green, but closer inspection reveals subtly different shades and textures. Pink and red geraniums and gold and orange miniature hibiscus add a punch of color.

Southwestern architecture is renowned for its courtyards, where Spanish Revival architects and builders made extensive use of architectural landscape structures such as retaining walls, benches, and fountains. This is one reason these homes relate so well to their sites. Most courtyards, of course, are relegated to the more private and secluded area in back of the house. In these two homes, both built in the 1920s, courtyard-like constructions of sculpted walls and planters expand the outdoor living area at the front of the home.

(top) A spacious interior courtyard, partly paved in clay tile and partly planted with grass, provides the focal point for this San Diego home designed by Clifford May, pioneer of the California Ranch House and built in 1933. All of the home's living quarters can be accessed through the courtyard. Ahead and slightly to the left, wide doors lead to a gallery that accesses the front door, bedrooms, and living room. Behind the camera is a door leading to the kitchen and utility area. May cleverly designed the wall on the right with a barrel-tiled cap and false pediment to look like part of the house, but it is simply a wall that parallels the property line. The vivid blue trim color was a favorite for Spanish Revival homes of the era.

(bottom) The courtyard of this 1929 Monterey-style home in Chico, California, evokes the grandeur of the California mission courtyards. Monterey style refers to a type of balcony usually attached to the front of a two-story Spanish-style home. This style was first seen in Monterey, California, in 1835 when a merchant from Boston added a balcony similar to those seen in New England to a Spanish-style house. The west-facing house shades the courtyard in late afternoon, providing space for social activities out of the searing summertime sun.

The fountain of the Chico home on the previous page has a classic octagonal design lined with hand-painted ceramic tiles high enough to provide seating.

(opposite, top) Some of the most sumptuous private-residence courtyards are at the Adamson House in Malibu, California (now open to the public). Built from 1929 to 1930 as a beach cottage in the Spanish Colonial Revival style, the home is best known as a showcase for the extraordinary tile manufactured by the Malibu Potteries Company. The Adamson house is truly a feast for the eyes. The front courtyard can be glimpsed through the wide front gate that is an entry point for pedestrians as well as automobiles. The high walls around the entry of the courtyard help define the home's footprint of living area. A slightly lower wall on the right and out of view is short enough to afford a view of Malibu Lagoon and the Pacific Ocean beyond.

(opposite, bottom) A lawn interspersed with random flagstone comprises the paving of the large front courtyard. The wall on the right buffets the wind coming off the Pacific but is low enough to provide a splendid view of the ocean. The entry to the house is deeply recessed and lined with tile that sets the tone for the rest of the structure. On the left is the garage, which now serves as an office and the assembly point for guided tours.

Drawing its palette from the ocean beyond, the courtyard fountain at the Adamson House is among the most beautiful assemblages of Malibu tile. The intermittent touches of blue in the clay-tile patio floor serve to introduce the fountain's dominant color, while the band of white on the pool curbing ties the design to the plain stucco walls on either side. Superbly painted peacocks flank the lustrous, blue-glazed central urn, whose mouth issues an unending supply of water that flows to the small basin beneath it, where it finally cascades through five runnels into the semicircular pool below. Whether by design or mistake, one of the tiles is upside down (hint: it's on the left side).

(opposite, top) Through ingenious design, the courtyard's complex elements and clean lines work together to become an integrated whole. The original plans for the house called for a fountain sited in a more traditional place—the center of the courtyard.

(opposite, bottom) A small courtyard off to the right of the front entry sports an outdoor fireplace, the same hexagonal tile as the back courtyard, and another fantastic creation using ceramic Malibu tile. The Adamson House didn't have central heating; thus, all the rooms, including two of the courtyards, had their own fireplaces.

The rear elevation of the Adamson House provides a showcase for more Malibu Potteries products: the faces of the living and dining rooms wings are completely tiled, and complementary tiles cover the planters boxes fronting the pointed-arch windows. Individual pieces of decorative tile surround the pair of French doors that open onto the patio, while directly above the doors hangs a large faience medallion. In the corner beneath the balcony resides one of the home's two outdoor fireplaces. A low wall on the left helps enclose the patio and turns it into a courtyard.

Renowned Arts and Crafts architects Charles and Henry Greene designed the two-story interior courtyard of the Duncan-Irwin House in Pasadena, California. At the center of the courtyard is a raised lily pond embellished with stylized art-glass water lilies. A Ficus benjamina *climbs towards an overhanging trellis on the second story, which acts as an additional shade feature as well as an architectural element. The courtyard came into being when the Greenes created a second story during a 1906 remodel. Their design allows access to the rest of the house from all four sides of the courtyard. The door on the right leads to the kitchen and dining area and the center door leads to a vestibule that connects the living and dining rooms.*

This bungalow courtyard in San Diego, is cleverly tucked between the house at the far left, an addition to the house at the center, and a painting studio at the right. The Japanese embellishments on the craftsman bungalow, such as the peaks on the gables, are echoed in the courtyard design. The Japanese influences seen in the courtyard are the lanterns above the door, the dry creek, the bridge of restrained simplicity, and the diminutive plantings that include heavenly bamboo, ferns, and potted palms.

(right) The design palette of this courtyard, created around 1900 in Santa Monica, California, is amazingly simple: bricks, pots, and plants. The house sits on a very busy street, and in order to make the front yard usable, a courtyard was created by means of a high wooden fence around the perimeter of the front yard. The carefully placed potted plants, the trained foliage along the eaves, the paved brick on the same level as the floor of the house, and the large openings afforded by the French doors make this courtyard a part of the house rather than a separate outdoor room. Alas, this courtyard and the house are no more; they were torn down a few days after the photograph was taken.

Originally grass, this elegant courtyard near Balboa Park in San Diego
is paved in French terra-cotta tiles
and enclosed with an ivy espalier
trained in a diamond pattern on a
six-foot-high wall. The 22-by-15-
foot proportions of the courtyard
make it large enough for parties
but small enough to provide a sense
of intimacy. A gate on the left leads
to a much larger garden and pool
area. Recently, the homeowner
added new plantings in the court-
yard but used plants that were sympathetic to Sessions' original design. A large camellia, part of the
original landscaping scheme, was integrated into the new plan Two large pots planted with seasonal
flowers and agapanthus next to the wall frame a wooden bench.

(opposite) A gently curving arch frames a view of the courtyard. The Colonial Revival home was
designed by famed San Diego architect William Templeton Johnson in 1920. San Diego horticulturist
Kate Sessions has been credited with the garden and courtyard design.

An original Malibu tile fountain in the Balboa Park courtyard supplies the necessary water element. The fountain is planted with lilies and water iris; large goldfish enliven it and keep mosquitoes at bay.

A green-patinated bronze frog, designed and sculpted by a local artisan, provides aeration to the water.

This sunroom links the courtyard to the house and provides a perfect spot to enjoy a relaxing meal while enjoying the beauty of the courtyard. A new trellis, positioned to provide a soft transitional area from the inside to the outside, will eventually be completely covered in wisteria. The indoor-outdoor feel of the sunroom is further enhanced by large glass doors that completely disappear into wall pockets. On the right is a climbing rose trained on an antique iron gate.

The courtyard of this Storybook-style home in Oakland, California, can be accessed from a curving gallery hallway at the center, the living room at the left, and a kitchen/breakfast room at the right. The columns, with their bulging barrel shape, or entasis, defy the usual constraints of brick construction. The monumental multitiered chimney with its curious lantern, an ornamental plaque of salvaged terra-cotta, and the unusual combination of slate and clay barrel tiles on the roof are all constructed to suggest great age, a hallmark of the Storybook style. Completing the scene are a whimsical clock, recalling those in European market squares, and herringbone brick paving, left without mortar so moss would grow to fill the joints.

At the M.L. Calvin house in Melbourne, Florida, bright hand-painted ceramic tile provides lively color throughout the courtyard.

(opposite)The Colonial Revival–style of the Calvin house was built during the heady real estate times of the 1920s. The two-story, nine-room house was originally used as a funeral home. The Colonial Revival style is quite boxy, symmetrical, and staid—qualities all befitting a funeral home. In the mid-1990s, new owners decided to liven things up by adding two cheerful courtyards. A fence and arbor frame the front courtyard, which is overflowing with an abundance of tropical vegetation. The courtyard is partitioned into separate sections that contain a secluded seating and dining area, planting areas, a pineapple-topped fountain, and a traditional porch.

The primary design element of the rear courtyard of the Calvin House is a large fish-pond decorated with ceramic tile and twin lion-head fountains. Lilies and elephant ears live in the pond, and on shelves above the pond dwell a variety of bromeliads. The rest of the courtyard is a showcase for a variety of tropical plants, all shaded by a massive live oak.

It's hard to believe that the quiet courtyard of this 1924 San Diego
home is near the corner of two busy streets. The homeowner partitioned this intimate space with the use of a diminutive
Japanese-style bridge that spans a tiny creek. Morning glory and
bougainvillaea form a colorful canopy over a meditation area
surrounded by heavenly bamboo, hibiscus, Indian fig, baby's
breath, and lavender. Papyrus, umbrella plant, water hyacinth,
and water lilies accentuate the water element.

CHAPTER 3

NEW COURTYARDS

ineteenth century Victorian homes had grand porches for entertaining and relaxing, and the Arts and Crafts bungalows in the early twentieth century were renown for their porches that often ran the entire length of the house. These features provided a smooth transition from the front yard or garden to the indoor living area.

In the 1940s and '50s, the front porch became smaller and smaller until it was little more than an overhang sheltering the front door. All social activity eventually migrated to the back of the house.

From the 1940s to the present day, the lawn has reigned supreme as the primary residential landscape-architecture design element. Certainly verdant green lawns provide an excellent platform to showcase the home, but they are mainly for show. Aside from the occasional game of croquet or badminton, lawns are for the neighbors to see and not for the homeowner to use.

Nowadays, many homeowners are looking for ways to recapture the indoor-outdoor lifestyle of a century ago by turning their lawns into courtyards or by incorporating courtyards into the design of new houses. New courtyards can be developed in a range of schemes, from ancient to futuristic. Creative designers have found ways to reclaim previously ornamental front lawns and turn them into living spaces. Backyard patios have been turned into fully functional outdoor rooms with the addition of lighting, appliances, and walls. These new courtyards not only enhance the aesthetic appeal of the home, they increase the resale value as well.

(opposite) What appears to be an ancient courtyard in Italy is actually a new courtyard in Calistoga, California, thanks to master trompe l'oeil artist Carlo Marchiori, whose showcase and home is called Ca'Toga. Here, he has created a veritable ancient Italian wonderland. Marchiori draws his inspiration from a number of sources, but the Venetian influence, specifically that of a Palladian villa, is clearly dominant. The side courtyard is topped with a wisteria-covered pergola that looks over the garden (La Piscina Romana) at right. The boundary at the far end is formed by the wall of a Roman pool.

The wall of the house that forms the north border of the courtyard at Ca'Toga is a canvas for faux archaeological finds and ceramic tile panels. Above the Venetian Gothic windows, a tile panel depicts the leonine animal attribute of St. Mark, the patron saint of Venice. A tile panel on the column depicts a bowl of polenta (Venetians are nicknamed polentoni—"polenta stuffed"), and bears the words se el mar fusse tocio e.i. monti de polenta (Oh, if the ocean were gravy, and the mountains were made of polenta).

(opposite) Ca'Toga's upper courtyard viewed from the opposite direction reveals Venetian Gothic windows on the far right with a dog-tooth (denti de can) pattern. Marchiori fabricated the windows by making an original in wood, and then taking a mold of it and casting the final products in cement to make them look like Istrian stone. The textured stucco wall is painted a bright oxide red like many of the buildings in Venice.

Marchiori's inspirations for the lower courtyard at Ca' Toga were the bath complex at the Villa Adriana, built by the Roman Emperor Adrian, the Villa d'Este at Tivoli, and the Bomarzo Gardens. Ninety-five-degree water, supplied by a well that taps into Calistoga's famed hot springs, is dispensed by four fountains. There are two small fountains in the floor (one out of view), one emanating from the breasts of the goddess Venus, which flows into a Roman bath, and one from the mouth of Hercules, which flows into a sarcophagus.

After passing through L'Arco di Pantalone, a pathway leads to a combination courtyard, grotto, and exedra (bench) that functions as a meditation area away from the main house. Fittingly, this combination area is decorated with odds and ends, leftovers and rejects. Mirror images of the words "illusion" and "delusion" face each other.

(opposite) L'Arco di Pantalone leads to a hidden courtyard. The arch was first carved in negative in wet sand and then cast in concrete.

A tromp l'oeil painting on the back wall of a courtyard in San Diego depicts a rural California landscape with rolling hills and orange groves.

(opposite) This magnificent courtyard was formerly the site of a small patio, deck, and lawn area. The homeowner transformed the area into a large 27-by-38-foot courtyard and adjoining dining area in 2001. The home, which was originally built in the Craftsman style in 1915, had undergone a number of alterations, including a conversion it to apartments and the addition of sleeping porches. The result of all the alterations was a home with a Mediterranean feel, a style that was continued when the courtyard was created. Highlights of the courtyard are the cast-stone pavers, soothing wall fountain, and rambling roses.

This canvas-covered dining area truly expands the idea of an outdoor room. The large, 25-by-26-foot space is used for entertaining as well as for a place to enjoy an outdoor meal. The table seats ten comfortably and there are adequate utilities (refrigerator, gas grill, cooktop, and sink) to prepare a meal without having to go into the house. Ample cabinets hold glasses, plates, and cooking utensils.

(opposite) The tidy 7-by-30-foot courtyard in this 1927 Spanish-style bungalow in San Diego is sandwiched between the house and a former garage that has been converted into an artist's studio. The courtyard was designed by the current owner after acquiring the property in 1998. Truly an "econocourt," this courtyard shows that one need not spend a lot of money to achieve an excellent effect. The courtyard has all the elements of a residential courtyard (four walls, a water element, and a seating area) in condensed form. A mission-style concrete fountain provides the requisite water element. Plants, all in containers on the concrete patio, are variegated yucca and impatiens (in the left foreground), ivy pelargonium (on a table in back of the yucca), Fishhook Senecio (the two long hanging plants on the far wall with the door), and fuchsia. On the back right side of the courtyard are pelargonium, impatiens, aeonium, fortnight lily, and gardenia. Bougainvillaea and variegated bower vine are in the front.

This pergola-topped courtyard in Solana Beach, California, doubles as an entryway between the street (through the door at the center of the photograph) and the house. It was originally built in a rather pedestrian 1950s style. The current owners wanted something that captured elements of a variety of historic styles of architecture. Thus, Spanish influences can be seen in the stucco wall, barrel tiles, and the terracotta pavers; the Craftsman style can be seen in the pergola; and the early American rustic bent-willow style can be seen in the furniture. The addition of a fireplace (on the far left behind the chair) turns the courtyard into a pleasant outdoor room that can be used all year.

This courtyard looks like it belongs on the planet Zorcon, but it is happily situated in Del Mar, California. Built in 1983–84, the courtyard, house, and grounds were designed by futuristic architect James Hubbell. Constructing two domes by inflating huge plastic bags and then spraying foam onto them created the basic forms that became the main living quarters of the home. Rebar was applied over the domes, and then the entire framework was coated with plaster. Other additions to the house connected the two domes, which formed the courtyard. The courtyard becomes an integral part of the house since most areas can be accessed from it or by passing through it. A fireplace and dining area built into the courtyard extends its use as an overflow area during parties. A sensuously curving stairway leads to a secluded study on the second floor.

The portal from the parking area into the courtyard (left) is a horseshoe arch. Hexagonal terra-cotta tiles and native plantings complement the organic form of the house and the courtyard.

Most homes built after World War II have outdoor living spaces oriented toward the back of the house. Gone are the large front porches seen on early-twentieth-century bungalows and the grand gingerbread bedecked porches of Victorian homes. The front yard in post–World War II homes is little more than an ornamental pathway to the house.

With a lifestyle oriented more towards the outdoors, many Americans are looking for ways to use the front yard while still maintaining a little privacy. One solution is the construction of a front courtyard. Lucas Lagoons created this courtyard on a street on Bird Key in Sarasota, Florida. The front yards of most homes on Bird Key are devoid of any outdoor living space. Lucas Lagoons extended the living area by adding a low, ivy-covered wall next to a circular driveway, which created a definite boundary between the domain of the automobile and the land occupied by people. The wall, the tropical plants in the garden, and the sound of water cascading down a small waterfall buffer the street noise and make the front courtyard a very usable area. Plantings in the courtyard consist of air-breathing bromeliads that ring the front, a foxtail palm at the center, triple adonidia palms, philodendrons, and variegated dracaena (Song of India), the bursting plant at the center back.

One of the most curious concessions to the automobile is the circular driveway. When these driveways are added to small homes, they render the front yard all but unusable. Pre-automobile, this type of driveway would only be found at grand mansions or commercial buildings that needed a smooth flow of horse-drawn traffic. Lucas Lagoons provided a creative way for humans to take back at least part of the front yard by creating courtyards in the small crescent at the center of the drive. In  this Sarasota example, the "walls" of the courtyard have been created with coconut palms, sea grape trees (Coccoloba uvifera), a variety of tropical plantings, and Florida limestone boulders. All the elements of the courtyard are formed in a curve, producing a soothing organic feel. The density of the plantings is sufficient enough to block street noise, which makes the courtyard a quiet retreat. The most interesting plant in the courtyard is the thorny "monkey-no-climb" tree (Hura crepitans) near the birdbath.

(opposite) The entrance to the courtyard is directly opposite the front door of the house, which was built in 1954. A curving brick walk through a grouping of sea grape trees allows a glimpse of the courtyard beyond. Riprap rock, a major design element in the house, borders the walk and provides a gentle transition from the house to the courtyard.

CHAPTER 4

WATER ELEMENTS

O f all the structural and aesthetic elements integral to the design of a courtyard, it is the water feature that gets the most attention from designers, architects, and builders. Like earth, air, and fire, water is one of the four basic elements that people are naturally drawn to. All cultures see water as a source of life, cleansing, and regeneration. Whether it's a still pond, a trickling birdbath, or a gushing fountain, the flow and transparency of water washes away stress and anxiety.

When designing water elements, architects are at their playful best mixing form, function, color, and motion. Architectural water features like birdbaths and fountains are available in a number of styles to suit the atmosphere of the house and courtyard. Water features can also be created by adapting urns, containers, glassware, and even pots and pans. The quality, complexity, and vibrancy of their creations are limited only by creativity and budget.

English jurist and author Lord Charles Neaves (1800-1876) described the well-executed water element in his verse "I'm Very Fond of Water."

I'm very fond of water:
It ever must delight
Each mother's son and daughter,—
When qualified aright.

(opposite) Rambling roses frame the wall fountain in this new San Diego courtyard. The homeowner rotates the plantings in the fountain with the seasons.

The earliest courtyards were built around centrally located cisterns and wells, such as this one in Colonial Williamsburg, Virginia. Once electric pumps replaced hand pumps and pipes allowed water to be distributed to any location, elaborate sheltered wells were no longer needed. Rather than abandon the wells, courtyard designers turned them into fountains and pools.

(above, left) Tile artisan Ernest Batchelder designed this elegant wall fountain in Seattle, Washington. Anything designed by Batchelder, and especially his tiles, are highly prized by Arts and Crafts enthusiasts. Indeed, individual Batchelder tiles have sold at auction for more than $1,000. Most of the tiles on this fountain are the plain mottled variety, but the surface is punctuated by a number of tiles with low-relief pictorial designs of flowers and fanciful ships. The arched top, stepped form, and scrolled corbels are design devices typical of Batchelder's work.

(above, right) A wall fountain designed by Arthur and Nina Zwebell sits on a tall stucco wall on a property line at the Patio del Moro in Los Angeles. The narrowness of the courtyard did not permit a central fountain like the Zwebells used on their other courtyards. Not only does the fountain provide the water element necessary to a courtyard, but it also breaks up the monotonous stucco surface. The trickling water enhances the serene mood, along with lush plantings of bamboo and banana trees.

(opposite) The ceramic tile wall fountain and lily pool at this 1923 Oakland home is faced with tile manufactured by Malibu Potteries. Real irises just past their bloom enhance the iris motif.

(above, left) Courtyard water elements have a functional origin, as demonstrated by this bucket and well found in Colonial Williamsburg, Virginia. (center) The gurgling water of a clay fountain installed in a bungalow court in San Diego muffles some of the street noise from the busy boulevard just a few steps away. (right) This triple-tiered fountain is a new addition to the side yard of a historic home in San Diego, California.

(opposite) A cast-iron fountain made from an urn offers the comforting sight and sound of burbling water in a New Orleans courtyard.

This fountain-birdbath in the front courtyard of a home in Melbourne, Florida, is topped with a pineapple, a symbol of hospitality. Pineapples became a hospitality symbol when early South American explorers returned to Europe and presented them to their patrons. Pineapple plaques are typically placed next to the front door, and sculpted pineapples can often be seen on fence posts in front of the house or other places that a visitor encounters before reaching the front door, such as this fountain in the middle of the front walk.

(opposite) This rare Victorian-era birdbath fountain was manufactured in the 1870s by Iske, a well-known East Coast manufacturer of cast-iron ornamentation. Typical of the late-nineteenth-century Victorian style, the fountain is laden with effervescent decorations, including scampering turtles and frogs. The diagonal bands of color on the column are typical of Eastlake style, while the pointed arches on the upper pan are a nod to Gothic.

An asymmetrical leaf-shaped birdbath (above, left) mimics the irregular shape of this courtyard in Sarasota, Florida. (right) This glazed ceramic birdbath at the Alexis Jean Fournier house (1915) in East Aurora, New York, is true to the Arts and Crafts aesthetic: its stylized tree trunk base and variegated green paint that mimics moss help it to blend into its environment.

(opposite) From the 1920s through the 1950s, it seems that no respectable backyard patio was without a brick barbeque. The advent of portable grills has rendered these brick sentinels all but useless, and most have been torn down or are crumbling away. This one in Seattle is a prime example of adaptive reuse. The former chimney is now faced in reproduction Bachelder tiles in a stepped pattern. At the center of the chimney, a large panel depicts twin peacocks. Additional Bachelder tiles adorn other surfaces, including a panel at the far right illustrating fir trees. Recirculating water runs down the wall and into a pool that was formerly the fire pit and onward to a larger pool with a border wide enough to double as a seating area. A variety of plantings, including blooming lilac on the right and evergreen clematis in the back, soften the hard brick surface.

A Grecian lady provides a continuous supply of water for this courtyard in San Diego.

Befitting the bar that invented the famous Hurricane drink, the courtyard at Pat O'Brien's in New Orleans boasts a fire-breathing fountain. The fountain provides additional visual entertainment with a continuously changing display of colored lights.

CHAPTER 5

BiG
WATER

Constructing a swimming pool in a small courtyard is a real challenge, but this pool/spa/pool house designed by landscape architect Brian Sublette in Metairie, Louisiana, manages to fit into a relatively small space without overwhelming it. The homeowner, well known for her restaurant designs, worked with the architect to create the eyebrow-shaped pool, which is painted a Mediterranean blue, and the spa, which features iridescent glass tiles.

The more traditionally shaped pool house and columned pergola are placed at an angle so, despite their angular form, they continue to flow into the curving design of the pool. The organic form of the courtyard continues with the scored concrete deck rimmed with tropical plants. A virtually seamless indoor/outdoor transition from the house to the courtyard is achieved by keeping the outside patio and inside floor of the house at the same level and by using the same columns on the house as on the pergola of the pool house.

A convenient shower is placed outside the pool house to keep the moisture level inside the Metairie, Louisiana, house at a minimum.

(opposite) In tropical Sarasota, Florida, the traditional swimming pool is giving way to man-made lagoons. The premier designer of these watery creations is Lucas Lagoons, a landscape design firm that turns ordinary backyards into exotic Edens. This courtyard lagoon, formerly a weedy backyard, wraps around a vernacular 1950s beach cottage. The homeowner wanted the lagoon's water to be devoid of any artificial chemical purifiers such as chlorine, so the lagoon is purified through an ionization system that adds silver and copper ions to the water to kill algae, bacteria, and viruses, thereby keeping the water crystal clear. The organic quality of the lagoon is enhanced with the use of beach sand at the bottom instead of concrete or fiberglass. Landscaping around the lagoon consists of coconut, pygmy date, foxtail, arenga, cardboard palms, papyrus, ferns, bromeliads, and other plants. Many of these species attract butterflies, a living enhancement to the tropical lagoon.

Oblivious that his fishing pole is missing, Tom Sawyer lolls away beside this Sarasota, Florida, courtyard lagoon, dreaming of adventures with his friend Huckleberry Finn.

(opposite) The high river-rock walls and abundant foliage help define the footprint of this pool, a recent addition to a 1907 bungalow in the Echo Park area of Los Angeles. These elements provide privacy and a courtyard-like feel. The shape of the pool, the adjoining spa, and the random flagstone paving enhance its organic quality.

The Roman pool at Ca'Toga (see pages 101–7) connects the side courtyard of the house and the lower Le Terme Adriane courtyard. The 12-by-40-foot pool was left unpainted to blend in with the rest of the faux ruins. River god spouts, cast-cement columns, broken bits of concrete to suggest great age, and a statue of Venus (out of view to the left) highlight the pool.

(opposite) This fanciful pool in a Storybook-style home in Oakland is located in a lower courtyard off the main courtyard. Although a relatively new addition, the pool is constructed out of artificially aged materials to appear decades old.

CHAPTER 6

COURTYARD LIGHTING

t wasn't so long ago that outdoor lighting consisted of a couple of floodlights mounted to the wall or a yellow bug light dangling on a chain. These lights were strictly for utilitarian and safety purposes, such as lighting a path or entrance. They were certainly not meant to create a mood. When homeowners started reclaiming their outdoor spaces, they found they didn't want to stop using them just because night had fallen. It wasn't long before this phenomenon was noticed by lighting equipment manufacturers and these companies came up with a host of modern illumination devices, including low-voltage lights, miniature halogen lights, submersible lights and solar powered lights. Well-placed lights enhance the plantings and living space in the courtyard and greatly expand the hours it can be used.

Homeowners and landscape designers can use combinations of lights to create just about any illumination level and set any mood. Many of these lighting operations are specifically tailored to the do-it-yourselfer, while others, especially those requiring the use of 120-volt fixtures, may necessitate the use of a skilled electrician.

(opposite) Cleverly placed lights illuminate the brick path and the lush tropical plants that lead to a concealed courtyard in Sarasota, Florida. Riprap rocks and sensuous sea grape trees line the path. The courtyard, accessed from the house after crossing a circular driveway, sits in the middle of a previously unusable front lawn.

The fountain, a new addition, was constructed of 150-year-old bricks found at the bottom of a cistern on the property as well as other bricks that were once part of the old patio. Illumination is provided by special submersible lights. The fountain plays host to a variety of seasonal plantings; seen here are grasses, iris, and taro.

(opposite) Rene Fransen's landscaping theme paid special attention to some of the homeowner's treasured plants, including this hundred-year-old boxwood that has been "bonsaied" to achieve a willowy effect. Special lighting puts the old shrub on its own special stage.

A playhouse that was constructed in the early 1970s for the homeowner's children enters a second generation of use for their grandchildren. Surrounding the playhouse is a massive gardenia on the left and plantings of miniature camellias and impatiens.

(opposite) This stately Greek Revival home in the New Orleans Garden District was built in 1851. The pavilion, erected from the remnants of an old carriage house, was added in the 1990s. True to the style of the oldest plantation homes of the South, the majestic columns are constructed of round bricks and faced with plaster.

In the early 1990s, a complete renovation of the landscaping took place under the direction of Rene Fransen, one of the premier landscape designers in the Southern states. Fransen paid particular attention to the lighting, which enabled the homeowners to entertain guests at elegant evening garden parties. Seen in the photograph is a large Japanese magnolia that shades the garden courtyard. Along the brick path are azalea, sasanqua, and seasonal plantings. The surrounding area is planted with a variety of native plants and the homeowner's prized collection of fourteen varieties of antique roses.

This miniature Japanese-inspired courtyard tucked into a side yard in south Pasadena comes alive at night, courtesy of some well-placed lighting. A small rock fountain is illuminated by up-lighting, while other up-lights illuminate the bamboo fence and plants. A fixture of the Arts and Crafts style lights the way to the courtyard, and another up-light illuminates an eerie clay tiki mask.

(opposite) Even the most modest lighting scheme can extend the hours for courtyard enjoyment. This courtyard in Chico, California, where summertime temperatures frequently exceed the century mark, is used more in the late afternoon and evening hours, thanks to a canvas cover and a few well-placed lights.

This San Diego courtyard is a veritable catalog for just about every type of outdoor lighting. Regular incandescent bulbs light up the walls of the house and dining area, outdoor floodlights provide overall lighting for the courtyard, low voltage lights illuminate the fountain, and rambling roses and plasma lights hug the steps.

SUGGESTIONS
FOR FURTHER
READING

any bookstores have a wealth of books devoted to plants and gardening resources for their local region and particular climate. The following books can assist builders and homeowners when designing a courtyard.

Blaser, Werner. *Atrium: Five Thousand Years of Open Courtyards.* Basel, Switzerland: Wepf & Co., 1985.

Douglas, Hardy and Sexton. *Gardens of New Orleans.* San Francisco: Chronicle Books, 2001.

Polyzoides, Sherwood, Tice and Shulman. *Courtyard Housing in Los Angeles.* Princeton, NJ: Princeton Architectural Press, 1992.

Reynolds, John S. *Courtyards: Aesthetic, Social and Thermal Delight.* New York: John Wiley and Sons, Inc., 2002.